HALLOWEEN DOODLES

Spooky Designs to Complete and Emma Par

RP|KIDS

PHILADELPHIA · LONDON

First published in Great Britain by Buster Books,
an imprint of Michael O'Mara Books Limited, 2009

First published in the United States
by Running Press Book Publishers, 2009

Printed in Canada

9   8   7   6   5   4   3   2   1
Digit on the right indicates the number of this printing

ISBN 978-0-7624-3760-3

Illustrated by Emma Parrish

This edition published by Running Press Kids,
an imprint of Running Press Book Publishers
2300 Chestnut Street
Philadelphia, PA 19103-4371

Visit us on the web!
www.runningpress.com

Draw the scary faces on the pumpkins.

Danger
Do Not Enter

BEWARE!! MONSTERS

Haunt the house.

What are the witches brewing?

Who is chasing the zombies?

Who is behind the mask?

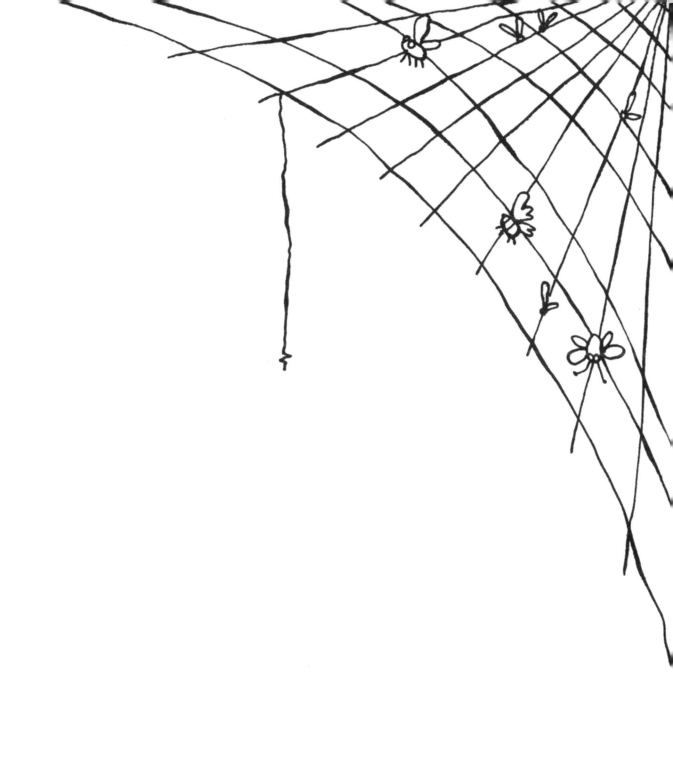

Draw a hairy spider.

By Mummy

1522

1601
MOORE

SIMPSON
1938

1901
FRED
is
DEAD

1952
BETTY BUTT

RIP
1328
I.B. NIGHTLY

Fill the graveyard with tombstones.

Fill the bottles with potions.

Oct 21 thur 2010

What is howling at the moon?

By: Daddy
Oct 21 tors 2010

Wrap the mummy in bandages.

Fill the wardrobe with scary clothes.

Paint the trick-or-treaters' faces.

Put some turrets on Dracula's castle.

What is under the bed?

Mommy

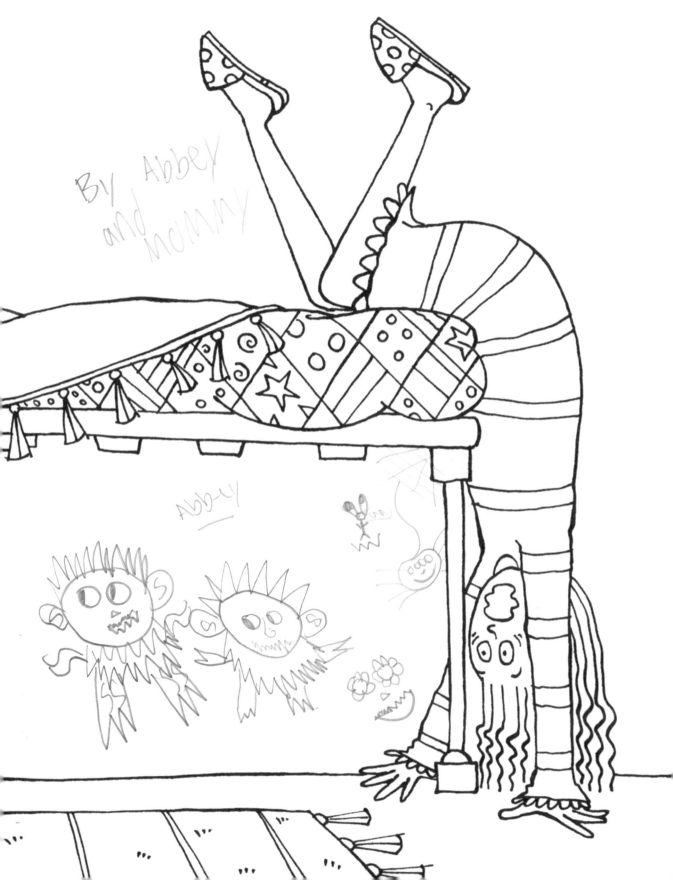

Fill the sky with storm clouds.

Give the vampires fangs.

Decorate the spell book.

Frost the scary cookies.

Portraits of the Monster family.

Decorate the witch's bedroom.

Fill the basket with treats.

Decorate these witches' hats.

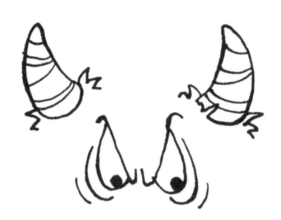

Run!

What are they bobbing for?

Write your own spell.

Give the witches broomsticks to ride.

Yucky monster stew.

Give Frankenstein's monster some scars.

Fill the room with webs and spiders.

Fill the witch's shelves.

Give the werewolves claws.

Sea monster ahoy!

Watch a scary movie.

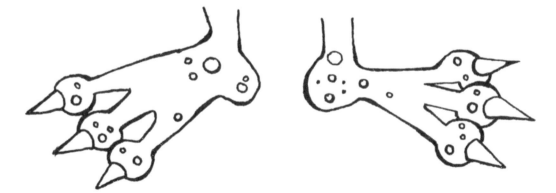

Create your own spooky monster.

Add more towers to climb.

Add a spooky door knocker.

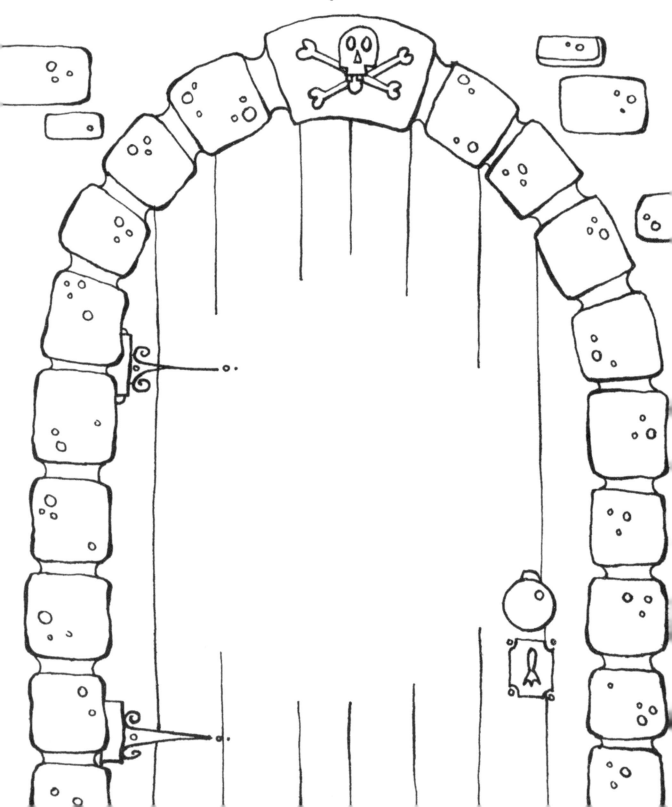

"Here creepy Kitty!"

Help her through the haunted forest.

Give "Frankie and the Spooks"
instruments.

Whose eyes are these?

Put the bats in the belfry.

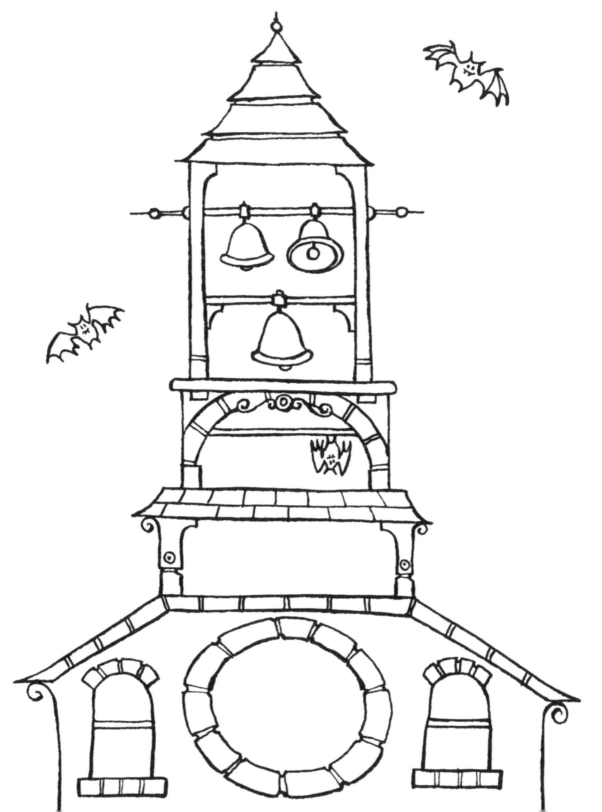

What is tapping at the window?

Nightmare!

Play some skull soccer.

Give us our bones back!

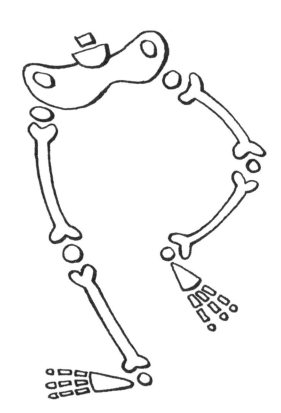